Women of the U.S. Army
PUSHING LIMITS

by Sheila Griffin Llanas

Consultant:
Francoise B. Bonnell, Director
United States Army Women's Museum
Fort Lee, Virginia

CAPSTONE PRESS
a capstone imprint

Snap Books are published by Capstone Press,
151 Good Counsel Drive, P.O. Box 669, Mankato, Minnesota 56002.
www.capstonepub.com

 Books published by Capstone Press are manufactured with paper
containing at least 10 percent post-consumer waste.

Library of Congress Cataloging-in-Publication Data
Llanas, Sheila Griffin, 1958–
  Women of the U.S. Army : pushing limits / by Sheila Griffin Llanas.
    p. cm. — (Snap. Women in the U.S. armed forces)
  Summary: "Explores the past, present, and future of women in the U.S. armed forces"—Provided by publisher.
  ISBN 978-1-4296-5447-0 (library binding)
  1. United States. Army—Women--Juvenile literature. 2. Women soldiers—United States—Juvenile literature.
I. Title.
  UB418.W65L53 2011
  355.0082'0973—dc22   2010033006

Editor: Mari Bolte
Designer: Juliette Peters and Kyle Grenz
Production Specialist: Laura Manthe

Photo Credits:

AP Images, 16, Rafiq Maqbool, 5; Corbis: Andrew Lichtenstein, 17, Bettmann, 9, 12, epa/Ali Abbas, 6, Lief Skoogfors, 19;
DEFENSEIMAGERY.MIL: SSGT Larry A. Simmons, USAF, 21, SSGT Stacy L Pearsall, USAF, 27; DoD photo
by Spc. Micah E. Clare, U.S. Army, 20; Getty Images Inc.: AFP/Patrick Baz, 22, Hulton Archive, 15, Hulton Archive/
Galeria Bilderwelt, 14, MPI, 10, Robert Nickelsberg, 26, Scott Nelson, 23, Time & Life Pictures/Cynthia Johnson, 25;
The Granger Collection, New York, 11; Library of Congress, 11; NARA, 13; United States Army Women's Museum, 16,
21; U.S. Army photo by Pfc. Scott Davis, 7, SFC Larry Johns, cover; Victoria Reischow, 32

Artistic Effects:
Shutterstock: Maugli

Printed in the United States of America in North Mankato, Minnesota.
092010   005933CGS11

TABLE of CONTENTS

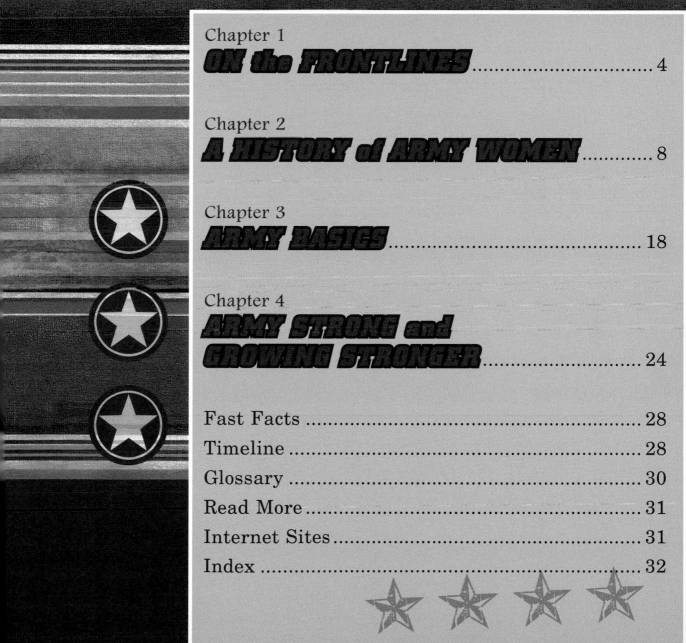

CHAPTER 1

ON the FRONTLINES

A Silver Star

In 2005, 17-year-old Monica Lin Brown was visiting an Army recruiting office. Her older brother, Jason, was about to **enlist**. That day, Monica made a decision that would change her life. She joined the Army too. After 10 weeks of basic training at boot camp, it was time for Monica to decide what to do next. A nurse's daughter, Monica chose to be a **combat medic** and give medical care to wounded troops.

In 2007 both Monica and Jason were **deployed**. Monica, then a private, was sent to Afghanistan. Her fellow soldiers called her "Doc." One day she rode out on a patrol mission. She was the only medic with the crew.

As their Humvee was returning to base, the troops were attacked. A roadside bomb struck the last car. All five soldiers inside were seriously hurt. Hidden enemies began firing on them.

enlist: to join the military

combat medic: a soldier who is trained to give medical help

deploy: to position troops for combat

Monica Brown planned on going to college, but she chose the Army instead.

Without thinking of her own safety, Monica grabbed her aid bag and ran across open ground. Bullets flew all around her. But those soldiers needed medical attention. She did not waste a second. "My muscles took over," she said, "and I started running."

Ammunition stored in the Humvee caught fire. The vehicle exploded. Monica shielded the wounded soldiers with her own body. She and another soldier carried the wounded men to a nearby ditch. Still under fire, she applied bandages and inserted IVs for fluids. There was no time to be afraid. Finally a U.S. helicopter landed and carried everyone to safety.

Women serving in the Middle East are often asked to serve in combat zones.

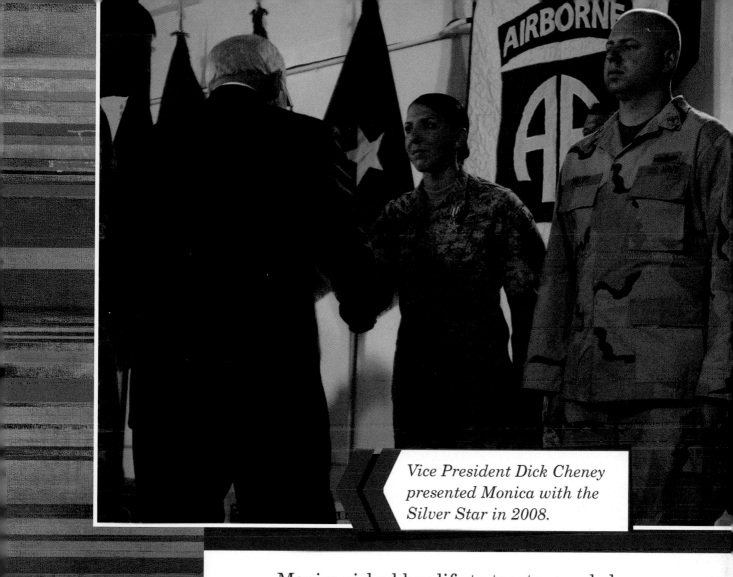

Vice President Dick Cheney presented Monica with the Silver Star in 2008.

Monica risked her life to treat wounded soldiers in battle. For her bravery, she was awarded the Silver Star. The Silver Star is the nation's third-highest medal awarded for heroism in combat.

In 2008 Monica was promoted to sergeant. She began teaching battlefield medical skills to other soldiers. Women like Monica make up about 15 percent of the Army. Almost 24 percent of the Army Reserve and 25 percent of the Army National Guard are women. Roles for women are still changing. "We are all making history," Monica said.

A HISTORY of ARMY WOMEN

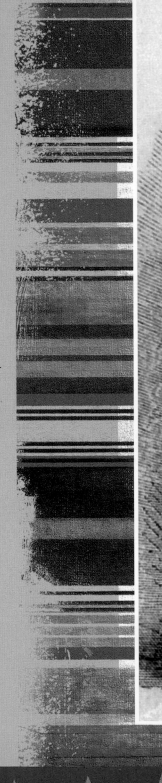

The Army is the oldest branch of the U.S. military. George Washington led the first Army during the Revolutionary War (1775–1783). Back then, women were not allowed to enlist. But they supported the war efforts by following the soldiers to the battlefield. These "camp followers" cooked, sewed blankets and uniforms, and treated the wounded.

Other American women served as spies and messengers. But Deborah Samson was determined to fight as a soldier. In 1778 Deborah joined the Army. She was tall, strong, and educated. It was easy to disguise herself as a man. She cut her hair, wore a soldier's uniform, and used the name Robert Shurtleff. Deborah fought for 17 months. During one battle, she was shot in the thigh. Instead of going to a doctor, Deborah removed the bullet herself.

In 1783 a doctor learned her secret. Instead of turning Deborah in, he took her home. There his wife could care for Deborah. But somehow it was learned that she was a female soldier. "Shurtleff" was honorably **discharged** October 23, 1783.

discharge: to release or dismiss

George Washington (center) ordered Deborah Samson's (right) honorable discharge after learning she was a woman.

The South needed volunteers for its army, but still did not let women serve.

Women were still barred from serving in the Army during the Civil War (1861–1865). But like Deborah Samson, some women dressed as men and fought on the frontlines. When women were discovered, they were supposed to go home.

But that didn't stop Amy Clarke. She signed up with her husband as a Confederate soldier. Her husband later died in battle.

In 1862 Amy was taken prisoner by Union troops. When the Union soldiers found a female prisoner, they were shocked. They returned her to the Confederate Army, but only after she put on a dress. The Confederate Army discharged Amy. She promptly changed into a man's uniform and returned to her Army post.

Jennie Hodgers, 1864

Northern women wanted to serve their country too. In 1862 President Abraham Lincoln called for 300,000 men to join the Union Army. Jennie Hodgers showed up. She passed a simple physical exam. The doctors only checked Jennie's sight and hearing. They did not notice she was a woman.

Jennie was assigned to an **infantry** unit under the name Private First Class Albert Cashier. Jennie served in the army for three years. After the war, she continued to live as a man. Upon her death, she was buried with full military honors as Albert Cashier.

infantry: a group of soldiers trained to fight and travel on foot

Jobs for Women in World War I

America entered World War I (1914–1918) in 1917. Thousands of male soldiers were called from their jobs to fight overseas. Without clerks, secretaries, and cooks, the Army turned to women as replacement workers. More than 25,000 American women served in noncombat positions in Britain, France, Russia, and China.

Founded in 1901, the Army Nurse Corps was the first official female army unit. More than 21,000 military nurses served during World War I. Another 1,800 African-American nurses wanted to volunteer, but were turned away. In 1918 the Army Nurse Corps accepted some African-American nurses to help with the flu **epidemic.**

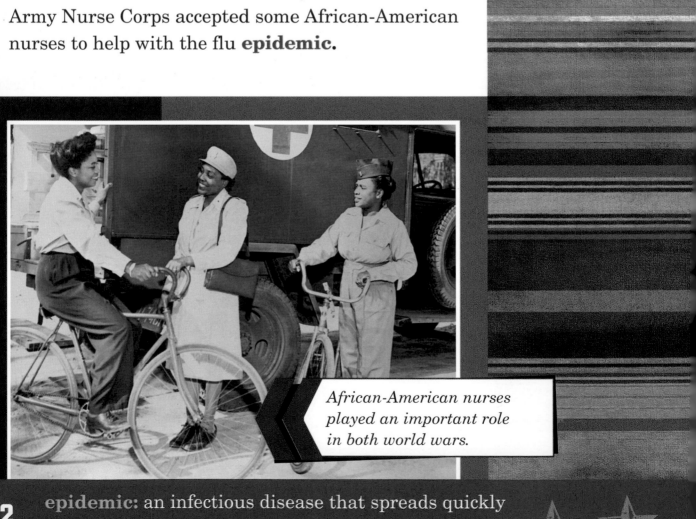

African-American nurses played an important role in both world wars.

epidemic: an infectious disease that spreads quickly

During the attack on Pearl Harbor, four battleships sank and another four were damaged.

World War II Changed Everything

The United States tried to stay out of World War II (1939–1945). But on December 7, 1941, Japan bombed a U.S. base in Pearl Harbor, Hawaii. Nearly 190 American airplanes were destroyed in the attack. After that, America joined the war.

Lieutenant Annie G. Fox was at Pearl Harbor that day. She was a member of the Army Nurse Corps. During the attack, two waves of Japanese fighter pilots flew overhead. Huge battleships exploded and sank in the harbor. Smoke rose in thick clouds from their decks.

More than 2,400 people were killed during the attack. Another 1,300 lay wounded. Annie and other nurses rushed to treat the injured. Ignoring the explosions and screams around her, Annie helped those in need. She also taught volunteer nurses how to care for battle wounds. For her efforts, Annie received the Purple Heart.

Members of the Women's Army Auxiliary Corps, 1942

Women worked hard in the factories and on the home front. But Congresswoman Edith Nourse Rogers believed women could be soldiers too. In 1941 she sent a bill to Congress to create a women's Army branch. In May 1942, President Franklin D. Roosevelt signed the bill, forming the Women's Army Auxiliary Corps.

In 1943 the Army made the Women's Army Corps (WAC) a full military branch. Women now had the same benefits and opportunities as men. But standards to join the WAC were high. Only 2 percent of the Army could be female. More women wanted to join than could be allowed.

Women in the WAC were code experts, radar specialists, radio operators, and mechanics. The Air Force was not yet a separate military branch. So women also served as airport controllers and noncombat pilots. More than 150,000 American women served in the Army during World War II alone.

The role of women changed after the war. Their service proved their importance in the armed forces. In 1948 the military created a separate corps for women. Female soldiers had permanent status in the Army, Air Force, Navy, and Marine Corps.

Army nurses served their country even after the war.

Nurses Are Needed Now!

FOR SERVICE IN THE
ARMY NURSE CORPS
IF YOU ARE A REGISTERED NURSE AND NOT YET 45 YEARS OF AGE
APPLY TO THE SURGEON GENERAL, UNITED STATES ARMY,
WASHINGTON 25, D. C., OR TO ANY RED CROSS PROCUREMENT OFFICE

Changes in the 1970s

The 1970s brought a decade of change for servicewomen in the United States. For the first time, women could become generals. Elizabeth Hoisington and Anna Mae Hays became the Army's first female brigadier generals. Hoisington was the director of WAC, and Hays was the chief of the Army Nurse Corps.

Doors continued to open. In 1975 women were admitted into military academies. In 1976, 119 women enrolled at the United States Military Academy at West Point, New York. Some men thought women would not last at West Point. Four years later, 62 women graduated.

Almost 900 WAC members served during the Vietnam War (1959–1975).

Today 15 percent of West Point cadets are female.

Recruits can become officers by following one of four paths. They can attend West Point. They can go to Officer Candidate School. They can go through a Reserve Officers' Training Corps program (ROTC). Or they can specialize in a field that could lead to an officer position, such as law or medicine. Officer candidates study military science and physical education. They choose an academic field like science or engineering. During the summer, they train for missions. Today women serve in 7 percent of officer positions in the Army.

By 1978 the Army no longer used the name WAC. Both men and women trained together and were given equal chances to advance.

17

CHAPTER 3

ARMY BASICS

The U.S. Army handles land-based military operations. Soldiers serve the Army in active duty, the Army Reserve, and the Army National Guard.

The regular U.S. Army is a full-time job. Members of the Army Reserve and National Guard serve their country and work regular jobs. They are called to active duty whenever the nation needs them. They train at least two days a month and two weeks in the year.

Soldiers in the Army Reserve serve under the U.S. president. Those in the National Guard serve under their state governors. Soldiers in both branches may be called to defend the country at home or overseas.

Army recruits must first go through basic combat training, or "boot camp." Boot camp lasts 10 difficult weeks. New recruits practice marching and learn to use gas masks and Army equipment. They handle rifles, perform field training, and go on night patrols. They also study drill and ceremony.

Today Army men and women go through basic training together.

After boot camp, some soldiers are deployed. Others study **aviation**, engineering, **intelligence**, or other fields. Within those fields, they learn Military Occupation Specialties (MOS).

Army medics, like Sergeant Monica Brown, train in harsh conditions. Medics practice to serve in real-life war zones. They run through mud in the rain. They jump from planes. They perform medical operations during practice explosions. By the time Army medics finish training, they are ready for any combat situation.

Monica Brown credits her Army training for saving the lives of her fellow soldiers.

aviation: the science of building and flying aircraft

intelligence: secret information about an enemy's plans or actions

Today women perform a wide range of jobs. All soldiers—men and women—are trained for combat. They are ready to face the challenges of the battlefield.

Army Strong

Female soldiers have proven they are Army Strong. Women served the armed services during Operation Desert Storm (1991). More than 24,000 Army women were sent to Saudi Arabia and the Persian Gulf. Female soldiers flew planes and helicopters on search-and-rescue missions. They drove trucks filled with supplies and soldiers. They guarded prisoners of war.

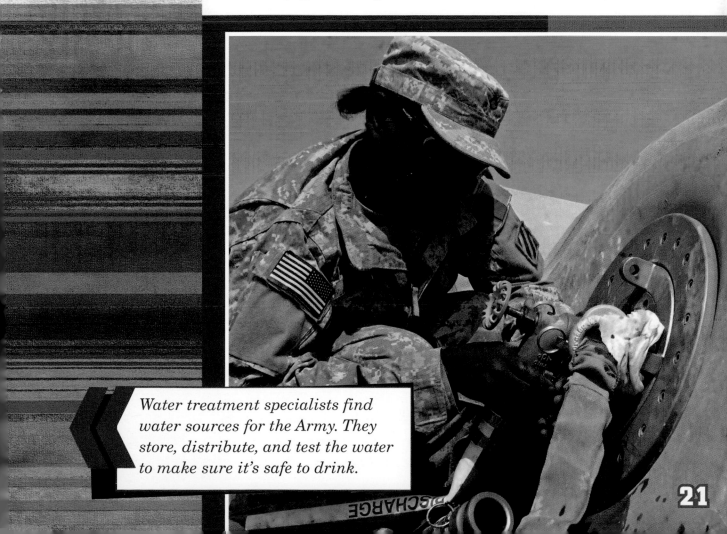

Water treatment specialists find water sources for the Army. They store, distribute, and test the water to make sure it's safe to drink.

After the Gulf War, the soldiers came home. People saw what women could do overseas and in a war situation. Women of the armed forces earned the nation's respect.

Hundreds of thousands of American women have served during Operation Iraqi Freedom (2003–). Between 2002 and 2007, women served 170,000 tours of duty in the Middle East. Today one in every seven active duty soldiers is a woman.

There are still some Army jobs women cannot perform. They cannot serve as tankers, in the infantry, or in the Special Forces. However, the war in Iraq has no frontlines. Women risk their safety to patrol streets, handle explosives, and drive trucks. The work is dangerous but rewarding.

Female soldiers prepare for a mission in Baghdad, 2004

But Army women can do some jobs that
men cannot. Male soldiers stationed in Iraq
or Afghanistan are not allowed to question or
search Muslim women. Instead, female soldiers
do this work. They search Iraqi women for
weapons at military checkpoints. They question
Iraqi women in local villages to find information
about terrorists.

Female soldiers build relationships with
people in the Middle East by doing their jobs.
They help people in war-torn areas. They
work with children in orphanages. They assist
families with daily needs such as finding food or
rebuilding their homes. The work is dangerous,
but female soldiers say it is worth the risk.

CHAPTER 4

ARMY STRONG and GROWING STRONGER

When the Iraq War began, Army women broke new ground. More women have served in the Iraq War than in any other war in U.S. history. In 2007 about 82,000 women served the Army in the Middle East. Women have learned new skills, advanced to higher ranks, and are stationed in all parts of the world.

Many female soldiers and officers have put themselves in the line of fire to serve their country. Like Monica Brown, Sergeant Leigh Ann Hester was awarded the Silver Star. She received it in 2005 for bravery in Iraq. Monica and Leigh Ann are the only two women since World War II to earn the honor.

Today women in the Army have reached the top of their game. In 2008 General Ann E. Dunwoody was promoted to four-star general, the highest rank in the U.S. Army. To date, she is still the military's highest-ranking woman.

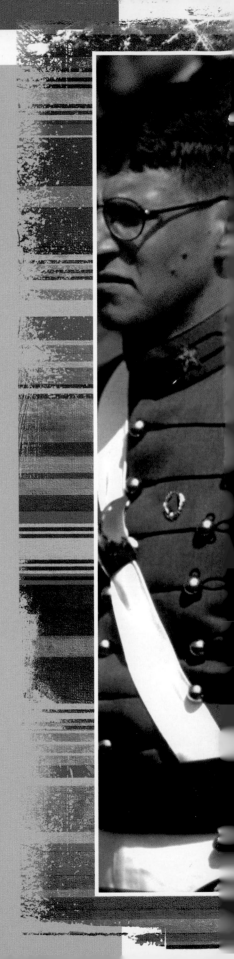

The West Point class of 2011 had a record number of female students.

Serving Away from Home

Serving in the military requires travel away from home. Soldiers are often stationed away from their families during deployment. This distance means leaving loved ones for long periods of time. Sometimes both parents are in the armed forces. They may be gone at the same time, but to different places.

Some children live with a relative, like an aunt, uncle, or grandparent, while their parents are away. Tours of duty are at least a year. Those in the Army Reserve or the National Guard serve an additional six months. For many, this sacrifice is a way to support the war efforts and to serve their country.

Today 50,000 Army women serve in Afghanistan and Iraq.

Honors for Army Women

Women have served the U.S. Army in every American war. Women now work in 90 percent of the Army's positions. The number of female soldiers serving has risen from 2 percent in the 1970s to 15 percent today.

In West Point's graduating class of 2010, 136 of more than 1,000 students were female. Two top honors were earned by women. Both the number one overall cadet and the best student were female.

At the 2010 graduation, President Barack Obama said, "In the 21st century, our women in uniform play an indispensable role in our national defense. And time and again, they have proven themselves to be role models for our daughters and our sons."

Women in the Army continue to take on new roles and challenges.

FAST FACTS

⭐ In 1983 Deborah Samson was declared an official Heroine of Massachusetts. The honor came more than 200 years after her service during the Revolutionary War.

⭐ More than 220,000 American female soldiers have served in Iraq, Afghanistan, and the Middle East since 2003. This number includes all military branches.

TIMELINE

The Continental Army is formed on June 14.

Congress creates the U.S. Army. Only men were allowed to serve.

Congresswoman Edith Nourse Rogers submits a bill to create an Army women's corps.

Congress approves the Women's Army Auxiliary Corps (WAAC).

1775   1784   1901 1941 1942   1943

The Army Nurse Corps is formed; more than 21,000 nurses serve. Another 25,000 women serve in noncombat roles.

WAAC is replaced by the Women's Army Corps (WAC). Women are given the same benefits as men.

⭐ In 1972 there were 12,260 women in the Army. By 1978 the number had reached 52,900.

⭐ In 1980 Andrea Hollen became the first woman to graduate from West Point. She was in the top 5 percent of her class.

⭐ West Point's class of 2011 had 225 women, which was about 17 percent of the class. This was the largest percentage of women for any co-ed class since 1980.

January—President Harry Truman ends racial segregation in the U.S. Armed Forces.

June—WAC becomes a permanent part of the Regular Army and Reserve.

July—The first women enlist in the regular Army.

The Women's Memorial opens at Arlington National Cemetery in Washington, D.C. It honors the 2 million women who have served in armed forces in America's history.

1948 1975 1977   1997 2001

The Women's Army Corps museum opens. It preserves and interprets the history of Army women in the WAC.

Weapons training for Army women becomes mandatory.

The United States Army Women's Museum opens in Fort Lee, Virginia.

GLOSSARY

aviation (ay-vee-AY-shuhn)—the science of building and flying aircraft

combat medic (KOM-bat MED-ik)—a soldier who is trained to give medical help during battle

deploy (deh-PLOY)—to position troops for combat

discharge (DISS-charj)—to release or dismiss

enlist (in-LIST)—to join the military

epidemic (e-puh-DE-mik)—an infectious disease that spreads quickly through a community or population group

infantry (IN-fuhn-tree)—a group of soldiers trained to fight and travel on foot

intelligence (in-TEL-uh-jenss)—secret information about an enemy's plans or actions

READ MORE

Alvarez, Carlos. *Army Rangers*. Torque: Armed Forces. Minneapolis: Bellwether Media, 2010.

Hamilton, John. *The Army*. Defending the Nation. Edina, Minn.: ABDO Publishing, 2007.

Micklos Jr., John. *The Brave Women and Children of the American Revolution*. The Revolutionary War Library. Berkeley Heights, N.J.: Enslow Publishers, 2009.

INTERNET SITES

FactHound offers a safe, fun way to find Internet sites related to this book. All of the sites on FactHound have been researched by our staff.

Here's all you do:

Visit *www.facthound.com*

Type in this code: 9781429654470

Super-cool stuff! Check out projects, games and lots more at www.capstonekids.com

INDEX

ABOUT the AUTHOR

Sheila Griffin Llanas has written
many Capstone books. She lives
in Wisconsin and teaches at the
University of Wisconsin-Waukesha
and at St. John's Northwestern
Military Academy.